The HeART and Science of Innovation

By Christina Enneking

"Much as your body is built from the foods you eat, your mind is built from the experiences you have." -Rick Hanson, Ph.D.

Published by Textbook Equity
Fearlessly copy, print, remix(tm)
"Making college books free or nearly free"
www.textbookequity.com
opencollegetextbooks.org

February 2013

For more information please visit
http://www.energyresultant.com/

1 ABOUT THE AUTHOR

After more than two decades of practicing yoga as a life enhancer during her corporate leadership positions, Christina Enneking founded Heart Happy Yoga in 2010 (www.hearthappyyoga.com).   In parallel, her consulting business, Energy Resultant, was launched (www.energyresultant.com), focusing on individuals and teams in coaching/facilitative sessions with an emphasis on innovation, mindfulness and customer-connection.   Christina has a Bachelors Degree in Mechanical Engineering from Santa Clara University and a Masters Degree in Nuclear Engineering and Business from UC Berkeley. Christina is a vibrant and knowledgeable yoga instructor, receiving her advanced Yoga Alliance certification to qualify as a 500-hour registered yoga teacher and is a Level II-certified Reiki practitioner. She integrates yoga, qigong, energy work, Thai yoga massage and lots of playfulness into her classes. In her free time, Christina has been known to shake a wild'n crazy shimmy with her husband, John, and children Carly and Will.

Philosophy Statement: *"I thrive on creating bridges between energy and rest, playfulness and intention, and creativity and wisdom. My passion is helping others accentuate their strengths as they evolve on their path to authentic success."*

2 ACKNOWLEDGMENTS & DEDICATIONS

I would like to thank many teachers who taught me such relevant lessons about life, leadership and the importance of following your dreams. Many of these teachers start with family and friends and I would especially like to thank my dear Dad and Mom who taught us to work hard, love deeply and laugh often. This book is especially dedicated in loving memory to my Dad, Charles Roberts, who inspired me to follow my passions in life: education, adventure, corporate roles, consulting, yoga and energy work, and fulfilling my heart's desire to serve others. I would also like to thank the many teachers in my corporate/consulting life and yoga intensive training, and particularly, yet not limited to, Kristin Cooper-Gulak, Jennifer Prugh, Gideon Enz, Donna Gardner, Saul David Raye, Erich Schiffmann, Shiva Rea, Tias Little, Kent Bond, Kira Ryder, Giselle Mari, Kelly McGonigal, Jonathon Littman, Michael Gaines, Brian Lawley, John Epperheimer, Bob Kriegel, and Bill Buxton. Without these individuals, the content and delivery of this information would be lackluster at best. These are the people who continue to extend their hands of service to teaching and helping many. I am eternally grateful to the people who continue to show up in my classes, workshops and coaching sessions – we are constantly teaching and learning from one another. Finally, I want to thank my supportive and loving family, my husband John and children Carly and Will. Without their laughter and patience as Mommy gets into tunnel-vision to finish her labors of love, I would not have the strong foundation with which to write, teach and share an abundance of love.   I now understand with meaning what my dear sweet Grandma Sheila used to say, *"I truly have the most wonderful life a person could ever imagine."*

With Love and Gratitude,
Christina Enneking
Los Gatos, California USA

Table of Contents

3 INTRODUCTION AND PURPOSE

The brain is the powerful command center for the body, housing billions of neurons that connect the physical, emotional and spiritual bodies of a being. The intention of this paper and associated workshop is to explore the workings of the brain from a neuroscience perspective, compare western and eastern approaches to the connection of mind and body, and to offer actions for cultivating and sustaining creativity, innovation and winning ideas.

Much of this work has been delivered to the corporate audience as well as yoga and meditation practitioners. It is poignant information for anyone who wants to cultivate innovation or creativity in his or her life. Creative solutions are for every being. My hope is that with more knowledge and awareness of how neural foundations affect us, the more mindful choices we can make to create a joyful, insightful, innovative and mindful community.

4 ANATOMY OF THE BRAIN

According to psychologist Donald Hebb, "when neurons fire together, they wire together". Mental activity actually creates new neural structures (Hebb 1949; LeDoux 2003). The brain has evolved over thousands of years and with modern science we can now see what areas of the brain are activated under certain scenarios, the size and mass of different components of the brain, and what parts of the brain can be strengthened if we choose actions with intention. The brain is like a muscle, "the more you use it, the stronger it gets". Same goes for qualities such as self control (Baumeister and Muraven, 2000), patience, innovation, creativity and wisdom – they can be exercised with focused intention to cultivate and sustain desired choices for longer periods of time if we rewire our brains, from the inside out.

Scientists describe brain development as an evolution from reptilian, paleommalian, then neomammalian brain (in other words, lizard to squirrel to monkey). The anatomy of the brain as a physical organ has evolved due to adaptability and the need to outwit predators. The brain has developed from the bottom-up and from the inside out, often seen separated into four key areas along a neuroaxis. The reptilian brain consists of the subcortical region or center of the brain, located on top of the brain stem, and is responsible for simplistic, motivationally intense and instinctual behaviors. As time has evolved and survival tactics enhanced, the modern cortex developed. This area of the brain has great influence over the rest of the brain, improving our abilities to bond, communicate, cooperate and feel compassion/love. There are two hemispheres of the modern cortex, connected by the corpus callosum or hippocampus. The left hemisphere is responsible for sequential and linguistic processing and the right hemisphere responsible for holistic and visual-spatial processing. The parietal lobe, located at the upper back of the head, is separated into a right and left lobe. The left lobe establishes the body distinct from the world and the right lobe indicates where the body is compared to features in the environment.

The result: the brain undergoes a high volume of automatic responses at all times. It often responds with actions that indicate" I am separate and independent." Yet, in order to live within a social and cooperative world, an organism must metabolize and exchange energy/matter with its environment. Take one of the fundamental laws of physics: for every action, there is an equal and opposite reaction. Energy and matter can move throughout the brain and body for optimal balance and performance.

5 BRAIN PARTS AND PURPOSES

The evolution of the brain, in deeper detail, evolved into four main areas, located along a neuroaxis.

The brain stem sends neuromodulators such as dopamine throughout the brain to get ready for action. This is often referred to as the reward center or goal center of the brain.

The diencephalon consists of the thalamus (central switchboard for sensory information) and the hypothalamus, which work to direct the autonomic nervous system and influences the endocrine system through the pituitary gland. The hypothalamus regulates primal drive states (water, food, sex) and primal emotions (terror, rage, fear).

The limbic system evolved from the diencephalon and includes the amygdala, hippocampus and basal ganglia. One can consider this portion of the brain "Grand Central Station" for emotions.

The cortex includes the prefrontal cortex (PFC), cingulated and insula. These regions are responsible for abstract reasoning of concepts, values, planning and the "executive functions" of organization, self-monitoring, and impulse control. The cortex also includes the sensory and motor strips that stretch from ear to ear (sensation and movement), the parietal lobes (perception), the temporal lobes (language and memory) and the occipital lobe (vision).

These four regions work together. Overall, the lower levels typically orient and energize the upper ones that guide and/or inhibit the lower levels. In general, the farther down the neuroaxis a response takes place, the faster, more intense and more automatic it is. Higher on the neuroaxis, responses are less intense and more considered. For example, the cortex (most evolutionary recent) enhances the capacity to take the future into account.

We will take into account the brain's natural intensity when it comes to instigating creativity, which in turn is a very primal, childlike quality. We will also explore the connection between creativity as it connects with intuition for fostering innovative breakthroughs.

6 WIRING AND FIRING

Serotonin metabolism is the process by which the brain balances the necessary energy for survival. Neurons release neurotransmitter serotonin, and when fired, tendrils burst into molecules. Synapses, or connections, are created. Neurotransmitters, this burst of chemicals, are received from other neurons and these signals tell another neuron to fire or not. Neurons are the building blocks of the nervous system. When a neuron fires, it sends signals to other neurons whether or not to fire. A typical neuron can fire 5-50 times per second – literally quadrillions of signals traveling inside the head within seconds. No wonder a popular term for our what goes on in our brain is "monkey mind." After all, "neurons that fire together wire together." Neoroscientists and behavioral psychologists have studied and shown with modern technology that it is possible to rewire experiences in the brain to create a new reality. We will begin our exploration with this as a key building block.

7 EXPERIENCES AND THE BRAIN

The will to survive in the wild depended largely on a creature's ability to choose correctly whether something approaching was a friend or foe. Even today, humans approach and avoid mental states such as pursuing self-worth or pushing away shame. The human experience still draws a great deal from the circuitry in the brain much like a monkey would look for bananas or a lizard would hide under a rock.

Let's assume you are talking a walk and see something curvy on the street in front of you. This form is sent to the occipital cortex that handles visual information. Then the occipital cortex sends a representation of this image to two areas of the brain: the hippocampus for evaluation of threat or opportunity and the prefrontal cortex for a more sophisticated analysis. The hippocampus also compares the image to its "short list" of "jump first, think later" dangers. If a match, it sends a high priority alert to the amygdala. This emotion center of the brain sends a "Watch out!" alarm and pulses warnings throughout the brain and hormonal systems for "fight or flight". Meanwhile, the PFC has been analyzing this figure to determine if this is a stick or a snake. The PFC is what allows one to "pause and plan" before taking action. After closer evaluation, you determine the object is inert and only a stick. All of this happens within seconds. Everything experienced was denoted as pleasant, unpleasant or neutral and stored in the brain (primarily in the amygdala). It is no wonder that the brain is often considered as one of the most powerful super-computer in existence.

In the world of psychology, some counselors describe to their clients the three basic parts of the brain and how they influence behavior. It can be summarized as follows:

- Brain stem including the occipital cortex is like the parent brain. This is what guides instinctual or habitual tendencies such as self-protection.

- Amygdala is likened to the child brain. This is where emotions and memories are stored.

- Prefrontal cortex is like the adult brain. This is where thinking and analyzing take place.

Interestingly enough, when the amygdala is triggered by a perceived sense of danger or threat, the signals between the "child and adult" are severed. This is often why a cooling off period is required when emotional reactions are intense. When we say someone is "acting like a child", often that is exactly what is happening. It is important to allow the prefrontal cortex to have an opportunity to process a proper and responsible action, bringing the brain to a function of "pause and plan" rather than "fight or flight" and take responsibility for one's own thoughts, words and actions.

It's as if we live at the edge of a waterfall with each moment rushing at us. Even though we may already be at the edge, or ZOOP, over the edge and gone, the brain is forever processing what has just happened. "Getting upset about somebody else's thoughts is like getting upset about spray from a waterfall." (Hanson, pp 164). Our challenge is to be cautious about jumping to conclusions and attributing blame reactively. Imagine if you were relaxing in a canoe and you suddenly hear a loud thump and the canoe topples over. You come up all wet and see that two teenagers have snuck up on you and toppled the canoe. How do you feel? Next imagine this canoe tipped yet the cause was a huge log that had smacked into your vessel because you weren't paying attention. How does this change your reaction?

A powerful mind exercise is called "Ten Thousand Things". Relax and steady your breath, producing an even flow of inhales and exhales. Pick a situation where you have felt wronged. Observe your reactions: physical, emotional and mind. Now create some of the various causes for why this person may have acted in the manner they did. Consider biological factors, social pressures, childhood realities and major life events. Consider their triggers, values, hopes and dreams. Look inside yourself and see if there are any areas where you can relate or at least come to a deeper understanding. Notice how you can alter your perspective and clearly determine a proper course of action with clear thoughts, thoughtful words and mindful actions. The more we act with a clear mind and peaceful heart, the more compassionate culture we can create.

8 PREFRONTAL CORTEX … A CASE OF WILLPOWER LOST

Psychologists continue to refer to the case of Phineas Gage when discussing the role of the prefrontal cortex for self-control. The backdrop of the story is year 1848 when a twenty-five year old foreman for a gang of rail workers was injured. Before his injury, his friends, family and acquaintances described him as quiet, respectful and strong in mind and body. He was said to "posses an iron will and an iron frame." (McGonigal, pp. 14-16). While on the job, Gage and his men were using explosives to clear a path through Vermont for the Rutland and Burlingham Railroad. Gage's job was to set up each explosion. Something went wrong and the explosion happened too soon, sending a three-foot, seven-inch tamping iron straight into Gage's skull. It pierced his left check, blew through his prefrontal cortex, and landed thirty yards behind him, carrying some of his brain's gray matter with it.

Amazingly, he did not die. His physician patched him up and replaced the largest fragments of skull with what was recovered from the accident site, stretching the scalp to cover his wounds. Within two months, he was feeling better and returned to his "normal" life.

What is most interesting is that although his outer wounds healed, something strange had happened to Gage's brain. According to his friends and family, his personality changed. Here is how his doctor described the changes:

"The balance ... between his intellectual faculties and his animal propensities seems to have been destroyed. He is fitful, irreverent, indulging at times in the grossest profanity (which was not previously his custom), manifesting but little deference for his fellows, impatient of restraint or advice when it conflicts with his desires ... devising many plans for future operation, which are no sooner arranged than they are abandoned ... In this regard, his mind was radically changed." (McGonigal, pg. 16).

From this early discovery to now modern-day studies, neuroscientists have studied meditation masters. They have shown on brain scans that those who meditate over extensive periods of time actually have created an enlarged prefrontal cortex, thereby creating a greater ability for logical reasoning, increased self control for making conscious choices, and taking actions today in line for a better tomorrow.

9 FIGHT OR FLIGHT vs. PAUSE AND PLAN

The instinctual tendencies from the base of the brain stem, or "fight or flight" responses, are what trigger action. The reptilian brain reacts to situations. Alternatively, the analyzing or decision-making center of the brain, the prefrontal cortex (PFC), can create a "pause and plan" response. Characteristics of both are as follows:

FIGHT OR FLIGHT RESPONSES

- Mobilization of energy

- Increased cardiovascular tone

- Inflammatory immune response

- Sharpening of senses

- Suppression of digestion, cell growth/repair, reproduction

- Prefrontal cortex inhibited

- Quick actions and reactive impulses

PAUSE AND PLAN RESPONSES

- Starts with perception of internal conflict, not an external threat

- Mobilization of energy to the brain, especially the PFC

- Slows down systems, decreases heart rate, blood pressure and calms breathing

- Increases heart rate variability (spaces between beats)

- Increases self-reflection and prevents automatic reactions

As may be concluded, the prefrontal cortex is paramount in the ability to grow our ability to make healthy and mindful choices. It's as if we have one brain, but two minds … the mind that is about impulse control and immediate gratification and the brain which controls our impulses to choose, foster and promote long-term goals.

10 FEMALE AND MALE BRAINS

Incidentally, the male brain takes longer to "cool down" once aroused or sensations of "fight or flight" are fired. This may largely be due to the differences in the brain as scientists are now finding. Research indicates that men and women have different structures and wiring in the brain, and men and women may also use their brains differently. In some cases, this may explain some of the stereotypes that we may not like to acknowledge about the genders. For example, men do score better at tasks that involve orienting objects in space, while women do better at language tests (Edmonds).

In 2001, Harvard researchers found that parts of the frontal lobe, responsible for problem-solving and decision-making, and the limbic cortex, responsible for regulating emotions are larger in women. In men, the parietal cortex, involved in space perception, and the amygdala, which regulates sexual and social behavior were seen to be larger.

Additional brain scans demonstrated the control group of men to have 6.5 times more gray matter in the brain than women and women with about 10 times more white matter. This difference may account for how men and women think different: men tend to think with the gray matter which is full of active neurons while women think with more white matter which consists of connections between the neurons. This may be why women's brains seem to work different for multitasking and enabling women to score higher on tests involving language and communication.

In addition, men and women access different parts of their brain when they think, as seen by imaging studies. In one study, men were asked to sound out different words. In the MRI pictures, it showed men relied on a small area to the left side of the brain to complete the task while women used both sides of the brain. However, both arrived at the same result.

Studies also suggest we can easily overcome biological differences, suggesting often how we perform is based on insecurities created in the mind. For example, girls' math scores improved when they were told that the exam was gender-neutral, while Caucasian men's scores on the same test dropped when they were told the scores would be evaluated against Asian men's scores (Crenson).

This research is simply interesting and what is most important in the findings is an enhanced sense of awareness and understanding. Practices where seeking to understand before being understood can create brain waves that create purpose-driven responses to situations and this practice is not reserved to any one sex or group of individuals, it is available to us all.

11 BALANCE

Whether male or female, the path leading to a fulfilling and healthy life lies in the path of our own awakening and self-realization. How much we know about how our brain influences our human experience and can help to reduce distress, dis-ease and dysfunction in order to create space for increased happiness, connection and acceptance of self and others. The brain has naturally evolved along a continuum from animalistic tendencies to human awareness and by recognizing how these functions allow us to process our experiences in a learning and choice-driven world, we can be benefit society as a whole.   The brain is a large contributor to how we perceive threats and opportunities and more research of stress ailments such as post traumatic stress disorder (PTSD) show how animals and humans differ. Animals (and the reptilian part of the human brain) "shake off" responses to dangerous situations for survival whereas *"we humans worry about the future, regret the past, and blame ourselves for the present."* (Hanson and Mendius, p. 12). One might conclude humans, compared to creatures in nature, are quite neurotic.

Each system in the body and mind must balance conflicting needs as the brain receives inputs and sends signals to the body for how best to survive. Human beings perform the following functions as a means of survival:

- Create safe boundaries or separation as we understand what is friend or foe

- Stabilize or maintain ranges within systems to allow for stability as well as acceptance of change

- Weigh risks and opportunities and decide how to process fleeting pleasures and inevitable pains

12 PILLARS OF THE MIND

Simplistically, the brain as it relates to the practice of increased mindfulness has three primary functions, or "pillars". They are:

1. Regulation

2. Learning

3. Selection

These functions can be expanded to include discussion as it relates to the ways our mind influences how we live our lives. These are primarily,

1. Virtue

2. Mindfulness

3. Wisdom

There are close ties between brain and mind functions as we explore the definition of each.

Regulation and Virtue

Virtue is defined as the regulation of actions, words, and thoughts to create benefits rather than harm to self and others. In the brain, virtue draws upon top-down decisions from the prefrontal cortex (PFC). Virtue also relies on top-down calming from the parasympathetic nervous system and positive emotions from the limbic system. Often virtue arises most when dealing with relationships and evolving to emotions such as empathy, kindness and compassion. When the brain is able to regulate its responses, the ability to make conscious choices by noticing thoughts and then choosing appropriate words and actions becomes available to us.

Learning and Mindfulness

Mindfulness involves the attention of inner and outer worlds. Since the brain is a learning organism, mindfulness is the doorway to taking in good experiences and making them a part of our fabric as well as learning from challenging experiences to promote rewiring of the brain and evolve reactions and triggers to chosen responses. The brain has an ability, through learning, relearning and unlearning to unravel experiences and create a reality based on intention. Once mindfulness becomes a part of the fabric of the human experience, there is less likelihood of living a life defined by past fears. One of my favorite acronyms for FEAR is False Experiences Appearing Real and it feels good to know we do not have to succumb to these if we choose a different path.

Selection and Wisdom

Wisdom can be defined as common sense, which can be considered a two-step process. When one understand what hurts and what helps, we can let go of what hurts us and strengthen what helps us. As a result, the mind feels more connected to all beings, more serene about how things will change/end, and more able to accept pleasure and pain without attachment to either.

The development of the brain is a fascinating story of evolution and adaptation to survive. When we look at the potential "poisons" in life, say for example the Buddhist view of suffering stemming from three poisons of greed, hatred and delusion, we can see how the brain centers contribute to a propagation of negative reactions. Virtue restrains emotional reactions that may have worked well in the past (for example, on the Serengeti!), Mindfulness decreases external attachment, and Wisdom cuts through past beliefs to arrive at a solution appropriate for present moment circumstances.

An example of how these pillars work in the brain is best illustrated with the story of blame – we'll call it "the Domino Effect". First, let's imagine you walk into a room and stub your toe on a chair that is in the middle of the room. You experience inescapable physical and mental discomfort. We'll call that the first domino: it's what occurred. Immediately, your brain starts to think, "Who put that chair there??" and you circle through all the emotions that stir up resentment or dismay about how you are the only one who cleans up anything around the house or how a certain person doesn't care about you based on their mindless behavior. We'll call that domino number two: what we create, often a greater sense of suffering. That suffering cascades through the body and stress hormones are created that trigger anger, frustration or other such emotional releases. Once we catch ourselves in this cycle, we can step back from the situation and consciously choose how we will react and what is real vs.

perception. It is key to step back and acknowledge what cultivates our own FEAR (remember that definition … False Evidence Appearing Real). Domino number three: choosing our thoughts, actions and words in a conscious manner. It is up to us whether we express the anger or realize it may be our own delusion that creates a bigger story for which blame is cultivated.

The key to rewiring the brain and creating space for awakening or innovation is to:

- Be aware of the facts and/or landscape of the situation

- Notice the tendencies of the mind and be willing to evolve toward breakthrough

- Stay grounded, then explore ways to take flight

With this strategy, evolution moves from unconscious incompetence to conscious incompetence then to conscious competence and finally unconscious competence. With practice, comes mastery of skill and each opportunity for mindful change can create a higher level of awareness.

13 BRAIN AS IT RELATES TO WILL POWER, COMPASSION, and CREATIVITY

Numerous scientific studies have demonstrated with MRIs (magnetic resonance imaging) how important the prefrontal cortex (PFC) is for cultivating a sense of "I will" or "I won't" decision-making (McGonigal 2012). Both are levers for self control and can be depleted as they pull from the same source, thereby limiting what a person can handle over time. Once exhausted, our source of strength for willpower, patience, compassion or innovation requires rest, recovery and replenishing if desired on a continual basis.

Results from some scientific and psychological tests include the following interesting findings:

- Smokers who go without a cigarette for 24 hours are likely to binge on ice cream (Duffy & Hall, 1988)

- Drinkers who resist a cocktail become physically weaker on a test of physical endurance (Muraven and Shmueli, 2006)

- People on a diet are more likely to cheat on their spouse (Gailliot & Baumeister, 2007)

Some studies have helped introduce strategies for what we can do to enhance or sustain desired characteristics. A mental focus test was performed on a control group and what transpired is the effectiveness of the following actions to replenish the willpower space in the brain. We can learn a rule or new task. In doing so, the learning mind is activated and ego/selecting mind has an opportunity to rest. Overall, recommendations for increased willpower, patience, compassion and innovation include:

- **Prioritize.** Notice what or where you are spending your energy and identify if there is a sense of over-controlling in any area. If so, there will likely be a weakness in another. Seek balance.

- **Create Structure.** When we streamline to commit to goals in advance, we can limit the demands on self-control. We do not get as caught up in the moment of temptation as long as our purpose or intention is strong. As we have less choice, our self-control experiences have less depletion. One definition of willpower, as identified by Kelly McGonigal, is "the willingness to do the harder things when it is consistent with a higher value/goal."

- **Restore.** It is important to replenish the control center for "thinking out of the box" or choosing the harder thing (such as reaching for carrot sticks over cookies). Tactics that have been proven to work include:

  o Enjoying "green exercise": going outside in nature and exercising in an abundant environment;

  o Performing creative crafts, handy work or playing a musical instrument: doing something calming, playful and allowing creative juices to flow;

- Practicing yoga, meditation or qigong: invoking slower breathing and a restoration of the parasympathetic nervous system);

- Getting sufficient sleep.

14 STICKS AND CARROTS

Perceived rewards can help motivate the brain and rewire experiences. Traditionally, negative experiences make more of an impact on survival than positive ones. The brain seems to have a negative bias. This can be seen in the human tendency to be drawn to bad news or have a shorter memory for positive experiences. The hippocampus actually stores negative experiences as information for future reference. In fact, studies show in relationships, it takes ~5 positive interactions to overcome the effects of a single negative experience (Gottman).

The Central Governor Theory suggests physical fatigue is in the brain and not in the muscles (McGonigal, referring to the work of Noakes et al, 2005). The mind expresses emotions of fatigue before the body or heart. This is often why we see triumphant examples of "mind over matter" or people demonstrating amazing feats as they describe "acting from the heart or for a higher purpose". A system of clear purpose or rewards can help immensely when trying to rewire the brain for changes in habits or thinking patterns.

Suffering can also be looked at through the lens of carrots and sticks.

- Greed: grasping for carrots

- Hatred: aversion to sticks

- Delusion: ignorance in seeing things as they really are

15 NEUROCHEMICALS AND THE TALE OF TWO WOLVES

The neurochemicals in the brain have a primary role in perceived awards and expectations of pleasure. Three key chemicals include dopamine, serotonin and oxytocin. Dopamine sends messages to the brain about pleasure. Serotonin plays a role in mood state. Oxytocin creates feelings of caring and cherishing. For example, in early stages of a healthy relationship, a higher amount of dopamine is released and pleasure centers of the brain are stimulated. Over the long-haul, healthy relationships exhibit a steady dose of oxytocin with occasional spikes of dopamine.

In the Buddhist tradition there is a concept of the 8 worldly winds. These can be seen as two sides of the same coin and include:

- Pleasure and pain

- Praise and blame

- Gain and loss

- Fame and ill repute

In states of greater equanimity, the winds have less effect. Similarly, as happiness becomes increasingly unconditional, the evolution of relationship grows. Connection and relationship are part of human nature, and they became a vital driving force for turning great ideas into innovative breakthroughs for the benefit of many.

Let's take the tale of two wolves. In life, there is the wolf of love and the wolf of hate (or looking at the worldly winds, being on either side of the coin). It depends on which we feed (Native American proverb). *"The wolf of hate gets more headlines, yet the wolf of love is bred to be more powerful."* (Hanson, pp 122).

The advantages of social capabilities and connection are arguably the most influential factor during the development of the brain. Apes and humans have developed spindle cells – neurons supporting advanced social capabilities and creating functions of empathy and self-awareness. Humans, due to complex neural networks, have more capacity for altruism, generosity, fairness, concern for reputation, morality, and forgiveness. Mirror neurons, which allow us to mimic another's behaviors, allow us to actually feel a sense of what another is feeling.

Insula and linked circuits activate when strong emotions arise. These mirror neurons develop around ages 3-4 and fully develop in the late teens/early 20's for humans.

As we become increasingly conscious in our behaviors, allowing for the wolf of love to be fed as we increase levels of oxytocin, the ability to see things clearly in the eyes of another becomes more accessible. When we are able to cultivate connection with others, innovation can flourish.

16 THE SECOND BRAIN

The autonomic nervous system is comprised of three components:

- Sympathetic Nervous System (SNS)

- Parasympathetic Nervous System (PNS)

- Enteric Nervous System (ENS)

The SNS is that which enacts our "fight or flight" instincts. The PNS primarily conserves energy, produces feelings of relaxation and contentment and allows us to "rest and digest". We need both to operate in a healthy manner: to think clearly and act in an appropriate manner. The SNS is what allows us to feel vitality, enthusiasm and passion where occasional spikes are necessary for being able to rise to challenging occasions. Similarly, the PNS is critical as a baseline for peace. The more we are able to calm the PNS in times of stress or perceived fear, the more we are able to rewire or control our mind away from perception and into the reality of the present moment.

What is fascinating is that on a physical level, the brain is not the only command center for the body. Scientists and doctors have discovered an entirely separate nervous system in the gut, the enteric nervous system. The second brain consists of sheaths of neurons in the walls of the long tube of our gut, or alimentary canal, which measures about nine meters end to end from the esophagus to the anus. The "gut brain" contains over 100 million neurons, more than in either the spinal cord or the peripheral nervous system (Gershon).

This system of neurons enables us to tap into our "gut feeling". The main purpose of these neural networks is to facilitate the elaborate function of digestion. As we break down our food, absorb nutrients, and eliminate waste, that all takes energy and chemical processing, mixing and a rhythmic flow of muscle contractions. The gut brain controls the digestion organs independent of the brain. Likely, human beings developed this web of nerves to perform digestion and excretion "on site" rather than through the brain and delivery of messages via the spinal cord. The circuitry is right next to the systems that require control according to Jackie Wood, Professor of Physiology, Cell Biology and Internal Medicine at Ohio State (Brown).

After further research, scientists have been shocked to discover about "90 percent of the fibers in the primary visceral nerve, the vagus nerve, carries information from the gut to the brain and not the other way around, according to Emeran Mayer, Professor of Physiology, Psychiatry and Behavioral Sciences at UCLA (Hadhazy). The second brain is actually a large driver for sending messages to the brain. Have you ever experienced the notion of getting "butterflies in your stomach" as a motivational driver for higher performance? Athletes talk about this motivation all the time. Or, have you felt that "inner voice" or "gut instinct" that is typically correct in its assessment without the mind's influence or overlays of information?

Newer research is starting to see ailments such as depression with a high correlation between brain and gastrointestinal turmoil. Today, one useful treatment of depression is actually electrical stimulation of the vagus nerve. The ENS uses more than 30 neurotransmitters, just like the brain, and 95 percent of the body's serotonin level is found in the bowels. Serotonin is becoming one of the key chemicals seen with a direct influence on anxiety, depression, irritable bowel syndrome, osteoporosis, ulcers, Parkinson's disease and possibly even autism. "It could start to explain why so many kids with autism have GI motor challenges in addition to elevated levels of gut-produced serotonin in their blood" says Gershon.

The digestive process begins when a specialized cell, an enterochromaffin, squirts serotonin into the wall of the gut, which has at least seven types of serotonin receptors. These receptors, in turn, communicate with nerve cells to start digestive enzymes flowing or to start moving things through the intestines. Serotonin acts as a go-between, keeping the brain and the gut up to date with another. 90 percent of this communication travels from the gut to the head via the vagus nerve (Brown).

"I have a theory that some chronic disorders may be caused by something like attention deficit disorder in the gut", offers Dr. Gary M. Mawe, Professor of Anatomy and Neurobiology at the University of Vermont (Brown). Dr. Gershon agrees—physiology is a large culprit of brain-gut dysfunctions. "If you were chained by bloody diarrhea to a toilet seat (reality for people with irritable bowel syndrome), you too might be depressed."

Researchers are finding that when animals are born in a hostile environment, their inner bodies program stress responses that stay with them in their future life. "Up to 70 percent of the patients I treat for chronic gut disorders had experienced childhood traumas like parents' divorces, chronic illnesses or parents' deaths according to Dr. Mayer (Brown). This may explain quite a bit about how healthy choices in what we eat and how practices that cultivate a healthy core, gut, or lower dantian (qigong and martial arts practices) are keys to health, happiness and well-being. There may be more weight to "we are what we eat" as it relates to both brain and gut functions.

17 EAST MEETS WEST

Age-old traditional practices such as yoga, meditation, ayurveda, qigong and most martial arts practices have long believed in a systematic approach to treat the body as a whole system: physical body, emotional body (often called "mind body") and spirit body.

According to Traditional Chinese Medicine, there are three-worlds in which we live:

1. JING (essence): physical existence. This includes the people, places, objects and molecules that fuel us and this world (lower dantian)

2. QI (prana): energetic presence. This includes the fields and/or spheres of energy or vortexes where we experience power spots, gateways or blockages; that which links matter and spirit (middle dantian)

3. SHEN (soul): spiritual world. This includes connection to spirit, higher purpose or spiritual belief/faith in a god. Many aspire to awareness, mind-control, intelligence and spiritual guidance (upper dantian)

In areas of practice our body and mind can be divided into these three realms as well. These three gateways are associated with physical vitality, baseline energy, creative energy and transformation.

- PHYSICAL: includes bones, tendons, muscles, organs, tissues and fluids. This is the base level or core of our physical being.

- ENERGETIC: includes breathing, emotions (often seen as the bridge between physical and spiritual), meridians/nadis, chakras, dantains (which move energy to areas or spiritual fields), and auric fields (think of pregnant women, newborn babies or people in love/dying).

- SPIRITUAL: includes thoughts, visuals, languages, beliefs, states of being (waking, dream, sleep), intention and awareness.

As we work through a physical practice such as yoga or qigong, we move the energy through our body and create a connection with breath and movement. Breath, also called "prana" or life-force energy, is the agent that works with and through us, much like water flows past rocks in a river or the flow of the ocean allows for energy to ebb and flow. When our breath is cultivated and thought of as a power house in the body, coming from the naval and flowing to where the body needs it most, our breath becomes like water, and creativity/innovation is birthed.

The combination of knowledge and practice are key to cultivating a desired future state. As my master Qigong teacher, Gideon Enz repeatedly affirmed:

> Proper Method + Consistent Training = Mastery of Skill

18 FIVE KEY YIN ORGANS AND FUNCTIONS (PHYSICAL, ENERGETIC, SPIRITUAL)

In Traditional Chinese Medicine (TCM), five key organs are seen as primary areas for health and well-being. Whereas the western view on medicine is on the function of the organ itself, the TCM view looks at the energetic system and integrated relationship with other key organs. The organs are associated with elements, or phases, which include earth, metal, water, wood and fire. We will explore the five key yin organs from a perspective of form, fit & function according to the traditional western medicine perspective and eastern physical, energetic and spiritual perspectives.

LUNGS

- PHYSICAL: The lungs are associated with the element of metal and are the densest and have the most magnetic quality that joins/binds the other energies together. The physical purpose of the lungs is to keep the blood in balance. Lungs are the organ associated with the respiratory system which includes external respiration (exchange of gases when outside and inside lungs with expansion and contraction), pulmonary respiration (exchange of gases to receive oxygen and release excess carbon dioxide), and cellular respiration (blood movement to cells and cells, in turn, dump toxins through the lungs).

- ENERGETIC: Lungs are the qi (air/life force) of the body and control the meridian channels and blood vessels. The lungs, as a yin organ, are paired with the large intestine (yang organ) and their instinctual function is to keep the body alive (breath is key!).

- SPIRITUAL: The emotions of grief/sadness are said to be cultivated in the lung organ when out of balance. The lungs house "Po" or the instinctual body, which coincides with our animal body to provide us the urge to survive, procreate and breathe. Think reptilian brain! When in balance, the lungs are known to produce integrity, purity, cleanliness and honor.

KIDNEYS

- PHYSICAL: The kidneys are associated with the element of water and are the yin organ that filters the blood and regulates the chemical makeup of the blood. They also regulate the water and electrolytes in the body. They are said to give us surges of power and energy.

- ENERGETIC: Kidneys are the foundation for all yin and yang organs. Kidneys house the transformative physical and energetic fire, or ming men, and assist in controlling the ability to eliminate that which has served its purpose. The kidneys are paired with the bladder as a yang organ.

- SPIRITUAL: The emotions of fear/loneliness are said to be cultivated in the kidneys when out of balance. The kidneys house "Zhi" or what is known as will, the ability to get things done, or the 'causing' force. Think prefrontal cortex! When in balance, the kidneys are said to produce confidence and wisdom.

LIVER

- PHYSICAL: The liver is associated with the element of wood and is the largest internal organ of the body. The liver is critical for metabolism of carbohydrates, proteins and lipids and helps to recycle nutrients in the body as well as detoxify poisons. Within the liver, bile is produced which is sent to the gallbladder for digestive and elimination functions.

- ENERGETIC: The liver smooths and regulates the flow of qi in the body. The energy expands outward like a tree and keeps the body strong and supple. This energy keeps us in balance with our environment and ensures harmony with our inner functions. This is also the energy which enables all nature to give birth and removes blockages from the meridians. The liver is paired with the gall bladder as a yang organ.

- SPIRITUAL: The emotions of anger/frustration are said to be cultivated in the liver when out of balance. The kidneys house "Hun" or what is known as the spiritual soul. Think intuitive wisdom! When in balance, the liver is said to cultivate love and compassion.

HEART

- PHYSICAL: The heart is associated with the element of fire and is an organ of all muscle. The function of the heart is to produce electrical impulses through the body through the SA and AV nodes, contracting atria and ventricles. In addition, the heart pumps blood through the body sending de-oxygenated blood in and out to the lungs and passing oxygenated blood in from the lungs and out to the rest of the body. The heart sustains chemical and biological processes. It is the heart which provides the warmth and spirit of life to all organs.

- ENERGETIC: The heart and pericardium allow for circulation throughout the body, transforming the distilled essence of food as fuel throughout the body. It is this spirit, or energy, which connects us to the universe and others, providing an avenue to consciousness. The heart/pericardium is paired with the small intestine/triple burner as the yang organs.

- SPIRITUAL: The emotions of anxiety/shock are said to be energized in the heart when out of balance. The heart/pericardium houses "Shen" or what is known as mind, spirit and awareness. Think compassionate self-control. When in balance, the heart is said to cultivate peace and a sense of order/understanding.

SPLEEN

- PHYSICAL: The spleen is associated with the element of earth. The function of the spleen is to stimulate the nerves and organs around the solar plexus and stimulate intestinal peristalsis. The spleen includes most functions of the digestive system and rules the muscles and limbs. It is the spleen that helps to move energy horizontally and in lateral and circular directions, similar to how planets orbit.

- ENERGETIC: The spleen processes digestion and transforms/transports food essence throughout the body. It is a contributor to holding organs in place and keeps blood in the blood vessels. The spleen is paired with the stomach as the yang organ.

- SPIRITUAL: The emotions of worry/over thinking/over analyzing are said to be energized in the spleen when out of balance. The spleen houses "Yi" or what is known as intention, visualization or imagination. This is the epicenter for creativity and innovation! When in balance, the spleen is said to cultivate a thirst for learning, trust and connection to ideas of greatest relevance in the present moment.

19 THREE LEVELS OF SHEN

In the discussion about the heart, it was mentioned the housing of "Shen", or mind, spirit, awareness. Even as we view the upper dantian, spiritual or SHEN world, there are three main levels. These can be defined as:

- SHEN ZHI: acquired mind; learned patterns or language; where we analyze, doubt and ask questions

- YUAN SHEN: intuitive mind, where we know what's going on without being told

- SHEN XIAN: awareness as it corresponds to the soul; our source of immortal light

In yoga philosophy, there are also three levels of awakening, as indicated by the sound often chanted in yoga practices: AUM (sometimes seen as OM).

- A: analogous with the conscious or waking state

- U: represents the dream state

- M: symbolizes the dreamless sleep state

Overall, many practices see the differentiation between three levels of awareness, awakening or even active living. We will now explore how Creativity can be cultivated and sustained and create a path to three levels of the innovative process:

- Idea: the seed of creative thought; initiating force

- Invention: process of evolving an idea into a useful product or process

- Innovation: ability to see and deliver value in order to serve the needs of others

20 THE ART OF INNOVATION

Throughout the past couple decades, I have had the pleasure and honor of working with top Fortune 500 companies in roles that demanded a strategic focus and emphasis on innovation. From early days at General Electric, under the leadership of Jack Welch on the Corporate Audit Staff, then in customer-focused roles under Jeff Immelt; to working as a high-level e-commerce leader at Hewlett-Packard under Dave Packard then Carly Fiorina; then becoming Chief Financial and Technology Officer at a telecommunications start-up, and continuing in multiple executive leadership roles at a think tank company for the electricity sector with the Electric Power Research Institute, the ability to bring innovation into the workplace was a critical success factor in my own career and within the groups I led. I would host "Simplicity Sessions" where the only guidelines were: solutions had to meet the KISS rule (Keep It Simple, Silly) and ideas had to cut work/time out of the day without sacrificing quality to the customer. In addition, I would facilitate Strategy Sessions annually, with follow-up sessions in between, to reflect on the past, develop line of sight for the future and define immediate next steps that could be implemented quickly under current resources.

Throughout the years, then later while consulting for businesses, I have discovered that people in teams play certain roles during the strategic planning phase. In the creative process, I see the need for the following innovation roles:

- EXPLORER: one who searches for new information and resources, and keeps a pulse on what is happening within the environment and new frontiers. The "futurist".

- ARTIST: similar to a child, encourages creative brainstorming in a limitless and free-flowing manner. Play and laughter are key.

- JUDGE: one who can prioritize and filter a high quantity of ideas into streams of consciousness and clear themes or like-groupings. Distills high volume of data into information to be acted upon.

- WARRIOR: possesses the motivation to get the job done; breaks strategic thought into practical pieces where action plans can be developed and implemented.

- STORYTELLER: skill of summarizing who-what-where-when-why and how solutions arise in order to create momentum, buy-in, line-of-sight from challenge (threat) to solution (opportunity) by way of actions; stating a high-level purpose that clearly resonates with customers as well as internal teams; promoting solutions or products to end-customers in a storytelling manner that resonates to the gut, heart or mind.

This approach is not foreign in the world of corporate leadership. After working with author Jonathon Littman, he describes the roles of Innovation into multiple personas as well. He co-authors a book with

Tom Kelley, the Chief Executive Officer of IDEO, one of America's leading design firms and notably one of the premier design firms recognized for their creative and innovative workforce and business practices. They offer eight crazy characters for hot groups:

- VISIONARY: the role of elder statesperson who inspires affection and enthusiasm amongst the flock. This is the person with a pulse on the current and future trends of the world and is most likely to figure out the "next" big thing.

- TROUBLESHOOTER: also considered chief problem solver. This is one who can see when politics or excessive niceness needs to be called out and projects put back on track according to the higher purpose. Clear thinking past clutter is vital.

- ICONOCLAST: one who disrupts the status quo or doesn't buy into everything. This is the one who breaks the mold and knows not everything fits inside a tight, neat box. Typically works well with the visionary and is able to spot key business trends and shares strategic insight for the future.

- PULSE TAKER: every company or team needs a heart. This is the ability to connect with others and see things from another's point of view with compassion or empathy.

- CRAFTSPERSON: skilled individuals in the field of creating and making product. It is critical to involve those who manufacture the proverbial product into the future-development phase. Prototypes can help morph ideas into inventions and potential innovative breakthroughs with an accelerated "touch and feel" approach.

- TECHNOLOGIST: every company needs the person or entity by which knowledge is key. This is someone who reads the latest journals, can unlock problems based on insight, and can point to seemingly obscure sources for wisdom that probe deeper connections between things.

- ENTREPRENEUR: one who is constantly experimenting, tinkering with prototypes and is a master of turning creating brainstorms into actionable realities.

- CROSS-DRESSERS: the bridge-builders in the organizations. Those who might have studied engineering yet have fallen in love with design or marketing. Passion mixes with capabilities and becomes contagious as these people help spread their passion like wildfire and invite others to the campfire of creativity.

21 SAND PILE THEORY

I do love a good read and I try to mix the content of my preferred books between professional development, scientific findings, new learnings/perspectives, and joy-filled inspirational stories. I often find certain content is delivered to us when we are most ready to understand it. "The teacher arrives when the student is ready." In the book, *The Age of the Unthinkable*, the author cites the work of Danish physicist and biologist Per Bak. He argued that if you pile sand, grain by grain, until it makes a cone about the size of your fist, how might you know when that tiny pyramid will tumble into a little avalanche? Can you predict when the sand pile will start to slide down? I found this concept groundbreaking when thinking of the creative idea generation process. Do we ever know when one idea will start snowballing into breakthrough or crack the individual/organization?

The sand pile theory brings to light the unpredictable nature of large systems. A single grain of sand can either trigger an avalanche or do nothing at all. Bak explained, "Complex behavior in nature reflects the tendency of large systems to evolve into a 'poised critical state', way out of balance, where minor disturbances may lead to events, called avalanches, of all sizes." (Ramo, pp. 48-49). He believed that sand pile energy, the energy of systems constantly poised on the edge of unpredictable change, is one of the fundamental forces in nature. He thought of the universe as a system of unmappable dynamism, one random grain of sand away from avalanche.

Scientists like to call systems such as this 'nonlinear' where the internal dynamics can disrupt the very system it is a part of. What happens within the pile is as important as what happens to the pile. Bak liked to quote French novelist Victor Hugo in saying, *"What if the real world is like this, precariously unbalanced between stability and chaos?"* (Ramo, pp. 54).

I see so many parallels with this concept and the world we live in. It is quite a precarious balance between stability and chaos, yet I differ in thinking the universe will all go to hell in a hand basket with one grain of sand. I believe we can change the odds in our favor by choosing, mindfully, a course of actions that promote stability over chaos. Just as we studied earlier, willpower, innovation, intuition and patience are like muscles where the more we use them, the more we start to move into unconscious competence and it becomes how we live. The sand pile continues to grow on a steady and broad base rather than a skinny pillar ready to topple.

22 PRACTICAL APPLICATION

It is important to point out these views are based on my own personal studies and embodiment of Yoga, yoga philosophy, therapeutics, movement, energy work, Reiki (Japanese healing), and Qigong (Traditional Chinese Medicine). Much of the work on Creativity and Innovation comes from personal practice as well as leading groups as a role of facilitator and consultant.

The essential map of practice has its roots in the system of yogic chakras, or energy vortexes, that circle throughout the body from the base of the spine (perineum area) to the crown of the head. I have seen how Creativity and Innovation can be cultivated, primarily in the gut center, yet when connection occurs with the intuitive center of the mind, Creativity/Innovation meets maximum potential for a clear and compelling solution that resonates with others. Instead of being a set of prolific brainstorms, these innovative ideas serve a deeper purpose.

STEP ONE: GET GROUNDED

The first step is to meet your authentic self, to know the brain has two minds and determine one's own recurring behavioral patterns or triggers. Get grounded! The question I like to ask is:

"Who are you when you're not trying to be somebody?"

In this first step, we build the basis for a healthy and strong foundation. We are able to see clearly those traits or strengths that keep us centered, whether as an individual, team or corporation. Signs of an unhealthy condition are a sense of being constrictively controlled, being self-centered, or exhibiting traits of ungrounded behavior. Balancing actions to strengthen this essential building block are to create a regular rhythm, invoke healthy consistent habits and to clear clutter/excess/complexity. In one word: simplify.

STEP TWO: GET CREATIVE

As one might think, the creative juices can start flowing as soon as a solid foundation is experienced. The second step is to start flowing with prolific brainstorming and building a steady and energizing basis for ideas to build upon. In terms of archetypical characters, this is when the creative artist comes out. Playfulness is key – and what we often find is that adults need permission to play. Grant it!

"The wise leader is like water ... cleanses, refreshes without distinction or judgment." (John Heider).

A healthy person or organization that can act from this "core" energy can cultivate creativity/innovation and see things streaming like a flowing river. Individuals or groups become more open to change and work harmoniously with others. In an unhealthy state, people can feel a lack of purpose or connection to others, a sense of overindulgence or a sense of polarity. Balancing actions are to connect with others (support network or even customers!), optimize core energy or competencies (build upon what you know), and learn to let go as you play and laugh!

STEP THREE: STOKE THE PREFRONTAL CORTEX

Once creativity has been unleashed, there comes a time for dedication and willpower to kick in. This is when goals are established or risk to reward trade-offs determined. When in a healthy condition, a person or organization is filled with passion, is able to shape the future to intended consequences, and has a reserve pool of energy or ideas with a strong sense of will/passion to get the job done. In terms of archetypal characters, this is when the warrior comes out.

"The intelligent want self-control; the children want candy." (Rumi)

We want to move past the mode of play and into action. Whereas this is the phase where motivation and persistence are key, an unhealthy condition is when there is an abundance of ego and people or teams experience a large amount of anger, frustration, stress and/or too much emphasis on power. Balancing actions include getting outside and integrating with nature, ensuring plenty of sleep and creating healthy habits (food, media and exercise intake), as well as focusing on deep breathing and mindfulness techniques.

STEP FOUR: CONNECT WITH OTHERS

Now that ideas have been framed into a logical game plan, it is time to watch and learn from integrating with others.

"The purpose of life is not to be happy. It is to be useful, to be honorable, to be compassionate, to have it make some difference that you have lived and lived well." (Ralph Waldo Emerson).

A healthy state of being in step four is a notion of interconnectedness, happiness and the notion that "we" starts to mean something. An unhealthy condition is a sense that voids are being filled with addictions, an experienced sense of coldness or instability, or a notion of operating at a frenetic pace leading to no results. Balancing actions include practicing random acts of service or kindness, finding ways to help/connect with others, and determining areas where abundance can flourish for a larger audience.

STEP FIVE: INVOKE THE COURAGE TO MANIFEST CHANGE

Many ideas get brainstormed and some shared with audiences with positive reaction. Many good ideas fall short of positive implementation based on a lack of courage to go the full distance.

Lily Tomlin offers, *"I always knew I wanted to become somebody when I grew up. Now I realize I should have been more specific."*

It is important for the communicators to rise and shine and express clear and compelling communication. Writing and idea promotion becomes key with the power of the spoken/visual word and stems from a healthy knowledge of product, purpose and placement.

Traits of an unhealthy situation are when communications gaps create obstacles to progress, when organizations or people can't seem to communicate issues and solutions or when knowledge is used unwisely or inappropriately. Ignorance is not bliss in this phase. Balancing actions include communication forums, allowing for "quiet think time", and sharing ideas in a non-threatening manner. Many techniques such as Mindful or Non-Violent Communication, from the work of Dr. Marshall B. Rosenberg, are wonderful tools to utilize.

In corporate settings and in personal coaching sessions, this is often when I introduce the rule of thumb to THINK before speaking. THINK is represented by:

- T: is it True?

- H: is it Helpful?

- I: is it Inspiring?

- N: is it Necessary?

- K: is it Kind?

Thinking before acting can be helpful. Particularly at times where dissent seems to be rising in the ranks, follow the process of: Stop, Ask, Introspect, then Do. In the wise words of Stephen Covey, *"seek first to understand, then to be understood."* In my own words, "THINK before a word is SAID."

STEP SIX: CONNECT THE DOTS

In order to create ideas that lead to innovative breakthroughs, the key is to develop prolific ideas, watch and learn from those whose needs you wish to serve, and then choose wisely. This is the step that takes incredible skill and insight.

Steve Jobs mentioned in his commencement address to Stanford University, "Have the courage to follow your heart and intuition. They somehow already know what you truly want to become."

A healthy condition exists when wisdom and the ability to "pause and plan" become highly valued and innate in nature. Visionaries are imperative as are finding ways to clear the clutter and entrenched programming of the mind. When Creativity/Innovation are connected with Insight/Intuition, the ideas that manifest are often golden winners.

Examples of an unhealthy condition are when people continue to repeat the same mistakes and/or excuses and may say "it's what we've always done" or actions become reactive. Cynicism can run rampant and typically there is a good deal of mind chatter or examples of unclear thinking patterns. When out of balance, recommended actions include taking time to "go out to the balcony" or stepping back from the situation to see things from a new perspective, unplugging or going on an offsite in a fresh environment, recharging and/or seeking neutrality.

STEP SEVEN: PUTTING IT ALL TOGETHER IN A BALANCED, WHOLE PACKAGE

Finally, the ability to create sustainable successes relies heavily on insight, serving a greater purpose, and connecting with others on a sensory level. Steven Johnson suggests in his book on where good ideas originate, "Innovation in nature and culture happens in an environment that is open vs. having walls build around it. Good ideas want to connect, fuse, and recombine." (Johnson, pp. 22) "The adjacent possible suggests boundaries grow as you explore them." (Johnson, pp. 31).

"Some people come into our lives, make footprints on our hearts and we are never the same. Build bridges, not walls." (Joseph Newton).

A healthy condition occurs when we are open, abundant, feeling fulfilled and able to connect the dots toward a higher purpose. It is in this state where we see our capabilities in way that can serve others. An unhealthy scenario is when we face extreme pessimism, are close-minded, and/or highly judgmental. Critical balancing actions include being a student and a teacher, invoking a practice where the higher good for others can be pursued, and allowing for trust to unfold.

23 SUMMARY

Innovation can be defined as the development of new value through solutions that meet new needs, inarticulate needs, or create ideas that evolve understood customer/market needs into value-added new ways. We all know when we are "on fire" with new ideas or a stream of consciousness and when we feel tired and haggard without a flow of creativity or innovation. By carving out time to practice prolific creativity, just like any hobby or skill, it gets easier and more innate. My hope is that these insights and the exercises within the workshop will help set the stage and stoke the fire of creative and insightful wisdom for ideas and mindful solutions to flourish.

In the words of Jeanette Leblanc, here is a motivational poem titled, "Go now, and Live."

Experience. Dream. Risk, Close your eyes and jump. Enjoy the freefall. Choose exhilaration over comfort. Choose magic over predictability. Choose potential over safety. Wake up to the magic of everyday life. Make friends with your intuition. Trust your gut. Discover the beauty of uncertainty. Know yourself fully before you make promises with another. Make millions of mistakes so that you will know how to choose what you really need. Know when to hold on and when to let go. Love hard and often and without reservation. Seek knowledge. Open yourself to possibility. Keep your heart open, your head high and your spirit free. Embrace your darkness along with your light. Be wrong every once in awhile, and don't be afraid to admit it. Awaken to the brilliance in ordinary moments. Tell the truth about yourself no matter what the cost. Own your reality without apology. See goodness in the world. Be Bold. Be Fierce. Be Grateful. Be Wild, Crazy and Gloriously Free. Be You. Go now, and live!"

24 EXERCISES

Reflect for a moment on the following questions:

1. What are you spending time and energy on? Is it fulfilling or draining you?

2. When do you have willpower, patience or innovation challenges? Identify when you feel most depleted or least motivated.

3. What restores or replenishes you? Make a list and refer to it when you feel weak or creatively challenged.

4. Metaphors are powerful tools for insight. Start by creating a metaphor for "the meaning of life" … examples include "Life is like a banana – you start off green and get mushy with age." Or "Life is like cooking. The outcome depends on what you add and how you mix it. Some follow the recipe and others wing it." You get the idea! Now create a metaphor for your current state in life … and from that, create a picture of your future state/self. What qualities/characteristics does the future state/self embody?

5. Which wolf do you feed? Playfulness/creativity/laughter or seriousness/judgment/ control?

25 SUGGESTIONS FOR CULTIVATING AND SUSTAINING CREATIVITY / INNOVATION

1. Create a clear and compelling intention or higher purpose/goal. Write it down and refer to it often.

2. Create motivational "names" or "labels" for your success and failure image.

3. Start by tracking or observing something you don't typically pay attention to (example: creating a budget draws attention to spending habits).

4. Do something to practice mindfulness (on a personal level, it could be something as simple as saying "yes" instead of "yeah", not swearing or texting while driving, or using non-dominant hand for eating, brushing teeth or opening doors.)

5. Learn something new. Feed your brain with the ability to learn, unlearn and relearn.

6. Develop a personal payoff or reward "carrot". What's the point of change?

7. Work with others – there's nothing better than finding ways to help/serve others.

8. Practice, keep diligent, observe where/when things get out of balance and do what is needed to invoke healthy habits.

9. Practice deep and calm breathing. Learn to meditate. Try yoga or a mindful movement practice such as qigong. Listen to music or play an instrument.

10. Go outside; get fresh air. Allow yourself some "blue sky" or "balcony" time.

11. Ensure plenty of sleep and plenty of play.

12. Laugh a lot!

26 REFERENCES

Baumesiter, Roy and Muraven, Mark. 2000. *"Self-Regulation and Depletion of Limited Resources: Does Self-Control Resemble a Muscle?"* Psychological Bulletin Vol. 126, No. 2, 247-259.

Brown, Brene. *The Power of Vulnerability*. Video on TED.com posted December 2010.

Brown, Harriet. *"The Other Brain Also Deals with Many Woes."* Retrieved from http://www.nytimes.com/2005/08/23/health/23gut.html?pagewanted=all&_r=0 on October 11, 2011.

Brown, Tim. *Tales of Creativity and Play*. Video on TED.com posted November 2008.

Covey, Stephen R. 1989. *The 7 Habits of Highly Effective People*. New York: Simon & Schuster.

Chuen, Master Lam Kam. 1999. Chi Kung, *The Way of Healing*. London: Gaia Books Limited.

Chuen, Master Lam Kam. 1991. *The Way of Energy*. New York: Gaia Books Limited.

Crenson, Matt. *"Remarks by Harvard President Supported by Some Experts."* Associated Press. Retrieved from http://www.livescience.com/strangenews/ap_050228_summers.html on Sept. 16, 2008.

Dispenza, Joe. D.C. 2007. *Evolve Your Brain*. Florida; Health Communications, Inc.

Edmonds, Molly. *Do Men and Women Have Different Brains?* Retrieved from http://science.howstuffworks.com/environmental/life/inside-the-mind/human-brain/men-women-different-brains1.htm/printable on December 29, 2012.

Enz, Gideon. Lecture notes from Qigong Teacher Training, *Part I: Introduction to Self-Healing*. Breathe Yoga Studio, April 2011.

Gershon, Michael D. M.D. 1998. *The Second Brain*. New York: HarperCollins Publishers.

Gottman, J. 1995. *Why Marriages Succeed or Fail: And How You Can Make Yours Last*. New York: Simon and Schuster.

Hadhazy, Adam. *Think Twice: Hot the Gut's "Second Brain" Influences Mood and Well-Being.* Scientific American. Retrieved from http://www.scientificamerican.com/article.cfm?id=gut-second-brain February 12, 2010.

Hanson, Rick Ph.D. and Mendius, Richard MD. 2009. *Buddha's Brain, The Practical Neuroscience of Happiness, Love and Wisdom.* New Harbinger Publications, Inc.

Hebb, D.O. 1949. *The Organization of Behavior.* New York: Wiley.

Kelley, Tom and Littman, Jonathon. 2001. *The Art of Innovation.* New York: Doubleday.

LeDoux, J. E. 2003. *Synaptic Self: How Our Brains Become Who We Are.* New York: Penguin.

McGonigal, Kelly PH.D. 2012. *The Science of Willpower, How Self-Control Works, Why It Matters, and What You Can Do to Get More of It.* New York: Penguin Group.

McGonigal, Kelly PH.D. Lecture notes from *The Science of Willpower* class. Stanford University. January – March 2012.

National Geographic, Special Publication. Until March 15, 2013. *Your Brain; A User's Guide. 100 Things You Never Knew.* Washington D.C., Time, Inc.

Olson, Randy. 2009. *Don't Be Such a Scientist.* Washington, Island Press.

Ramo, Joshua Cooper. 2009. *The Age of the Unthinkable.* New York: Little, Brown and Company.

Scientific American. December 2012. *World Changing Ideas.* Nature America, Inc.

The Brain, a Discover Magazine Special. Fall 2012. What's Really on Your Mind. Kalmbach Publishing Co.

Von Oech, Roger. 1998. *A Whack on the Side of the Head.* New York: Warner Books, Inc.proper method

ALPHABETICAL INDEX